Being a vegetarian

DEBORAH CHANCELLOR

W
FRANKLIN WATTS
LONDON · SYDNEY

First published in 2009
by Franklin Watts

Copyright © Franklin Watts 2009

Franklin Watts
338 Euston Road
London NW1 3BH

Franklin Watts Australia
Level 17/207 Kent Street
Sydney, NSW 2000

Series editor: Sarah Peutrill
Editor: Sarah Ridley
Art director: Jonathan Hair
Design: www.rawshock.co.uk
Picture research: Diana Morris

Dewey number: 179.3

ISBN 978 0 7496 8831 8

Printed in China

Franklin Watts is a division of Hachette Children's
Books, an Hachette UK company.
www.hachette.co.uk

CONTENTS

Look out for these features

IN FOCUS

A more detailed information panel.

ROLE PLAY

An opportunity to get together with some friends and each take a point of view and follow it through.

YOUR CALL

An invitation to explore your own feelings.

?

Dilemma

Focus on someone's difficult decision and think how you might advise them.

FOR! **AGAINST!**

Look at both sides of the argument and see which you agree with.

RESEARCH IT YOURSELF

Some topics that you could research yourself, either in the library or on the Internet.

What is a vegetarian?

 **A** vegetarian is a person who does not eat meat. There are different kinds of vegetarians, depending on the particular diet that is followed. However, not everyone wants to be a vegetarian. Many people enjoy eating meat, and would not want to give it up.

Varied diet

Some people think vegetarians only eat fruit and vegetables, but this is not true. Vegetarians can have a varied and interesting diet that includes many different kinds of nuts, seeds and pulses, eggs, cereals and dairy products.

Different vegetarian diets

All vegetarians can eat fruit, vegetables, nuts, seeds, pulses and grains, but they may add other things to their diet.

- **Ovo-lacto-vegetarians** eat eggs and dairy foods, but don't eat meat, poultry or fish.
- **Ovo-vegetarians** eat eggs, but don't eat meat, poultry, fish or dairy foods.
- **Lacto-vegetarians** eat dairy foods, but don't eat meat, poultry, fish or eggs.
- **Vegans** don't eat any animal products, including eggs and dairy foods.

Some people eat a diet similar to vegetarians but with the addition of some white meat, such as fish or chicken.

- **Pescetarians** eat fish, eggs and dairy foods, but don't eat meat or poultry.
- **Pollo vegetarians** eat chicken, eggs and dairy foods, but don't eat other meats or fish.
- **Demi-vegetarians** eat chicken, fish, eggs and dairy foods, but don't eat red meat (such as beef).

Nuts are a source of protein, and can be an important part of a vegetarian diet. You can buy them with their shells on and use a nutcracker to get at the nuts inside.

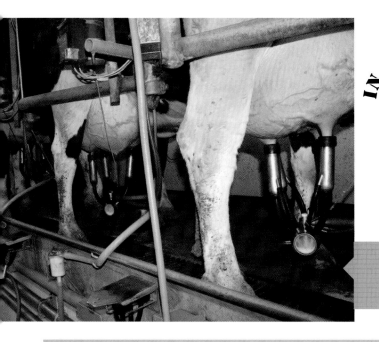

Vegetarianism

The word 'vegetarian' comes from the Latin word *vegetus,* which means 'lively'. It does not come from the English word 'vegetable'.

Milk and other dairy products are avoided by some vegetarians.

ARGUMENTS FOR AND AGAINST BEING VEGETARIAN

FOR!

- Animals have a right to life, and should not be killed for their meat.
- Many farm animals are kept in cruel conditions.
- Animal farming is bad for the environment because it creates pollution.
- Animal farming uses too much land and too many natural resources.
- A vegetarian diet is healthy, because it is low in fat and high in fibre.

AGAINST!

- If people didn't eat meat, nobody would look after farm animals in the first place.
- Meat and dairy foods provide important nutrients, especially for children.
- It is much easier for meat-eaters to have a healthy diet.
- Humans are omnivores which means they can eat plants and meat.
- A meat-eating diet is more varied and interesting than a vegetarian one.

Most vegetarians eat a good variety of foods, but meat-eaters have an even greater choice.

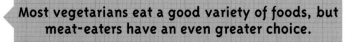

What is a vegan?

Vegans are strict vegetarians. They cut out all animal products from their diet, and do not eat eggs and dairy foods. Many vegans have a healthy diet, but it is harder for them to get all the nutrients they need. It takes time and effort to plan a good vegan diet, and this puts many people off becoming a vegan.

What do vegans eat?

Vegans should eat the following kinds of food every day:
- Vegetables (including green, leafy ones)
- Fruits (including dried fruits)
- Bread, pasta, rice and cereals with added vitamins
- Beans, pulses, nuts, seeds and protein foods
- Vegetable oils and fats
- Non-dairy foods with added vitamins (such as soya milk).

Missing nutrients

Some important nutrients can be missing from a vegan diet. Iron helps your body make red blood cells, and if it is missing from your diet, you can develop a condition called anaemia. If vegans eat plenty of green vegetables, such as broccoli and spinach, nuts, dried fruit, wholegrains and even seaweed, they will get enough iron. Other important vitamins are vitamin D and vitamin B12. Many vegans take supplements to make sure they get enough of these vitamins.

Kidney beans

Chickpeas

Cashew nuts

Almonds

Black beans

Red lentils

Peanuts

Sunflower seeds

Eating a variety of beans, nuts and seeds is important in a vegan diet.

Calcium

Calcium keeps our bones and teeth healthy. Non-vegans get enough calcium in their diet by eating dairy products but calcium is also found in green leafy vegetables, sesame seeds, sunflower seeds, almonds, and cereals with calcium added to them.

A balanced diet should give you lots of energy. If you are tired all the time, you may not be eating enough of the right kinds of food.

Many breakfast cereals have vitamins added to them. They are called 'fortified cereals'.

 Dilemma:
Your friend is a vegan. She is always tired and lacks any energy. You are worried that she is not planning her diet properly. What should you do?

ROLE PLAY: WHAT IS WRONG WITH EATING EGGS?

Vegans do not eat eggs. Here are two people's opinions on this. Can you take one of their arguments and follow it through?

1

"Eating free-range eggs is okay, because the hens that laid them were well looked after and didn't suffer during their lives."

Farmer, Francis Goodson

2

"Chickens lay eggs to have chicks, not to feed humans. Many poultry farms keep hens in cruel conditions. If no one ate eggs, these farms wouldn't exist."

Animal rights activist, and vegan Becky Metcalf

Animal welfare

Many vegetarians don't like the way animals are kept on farms. Some farmers keep animals in crowded spaces and feed them special diets to make them grow faster, have more babies or produce more milk. This is called intensive farming.

Free-range animals

Free-range and organically farmed animals lead more natural lives than those kept on intensive farms. The animals must be able to get outside, rather than being shut up in sheds or barns. However, the meat, eggs and milk from these animals can be more expensive, because it costs more to farm animals in this way.

 Dilemma:

Chris is a vegetarian student. He can't afford to buy free-range eggs and organic dairy foods, but he doesn't agree with intensive farming. Should he cut these foods out of his diet and become a vegan?

Some 'demi-vegetarians' only eat meat from free-range and organic farms.

These hens are kept in crowded cages on a battery farm.

Battery chickens

Hens in battery cages can't move or stretch their wings to fly. They never see daylight or breathe fresh air. Their feathers may be plucked out by other hens, and their feet damaged by standing on wire floors. Chickens that are sold for their meat may not be kept in cages. However intensively farmed chickens are kept in enclosed spaces without much room to move.

Do you think supermarkets should stop selling intensively farmed chickens and battery chicken eggs? Should the government ban this style of farming?

ARGUMENTS FOR AND AGAINST FARMING ANIMALS

FOR!

- People have the right to eat meat. Animals need to be farmed so that this is possible.
- Animal farming is a massive industry, providing work for millions worldwide.
- If animals weren't kept on farms, our landscape would change completely.
- People have kept animals for many thousands of years. Why stop now?

AGAINST!

- Animal farming is less efficient than crop farming and creates more pollution.
- Intensive farms keep animals in cramped and cruel conditions.
- Animals have a right to life, and to live in a natural way.
- Dairy animals produce milk for their young, not for people to drink.

Green vegetarians

Some people are vegetarians because they think this is a better choice for the environment. They believe that if more people were vegetarian, less fertile land would be taken and used for farming animals. Fewer fragile habitats, such as rainforests, would be destroyed, taking with them many endangered species. There would also be less pollution.

Forests or farms?

Lots of land is needed to farm animals. For example, large areas of rainforest in South America are being cleared to make way for cattle ranches, to produce beef for the US fast food industry. This is bad for the environment — rainforests absorb carbon dioxide, a greenhouse gas that adds to global warming. Fewer rainforests means more global warming.

IN FOCUS

Methane

Farm animals — mainly cattle — release a greenhouse gas called methane when they are digesting grass. This makes up 18% of all greenhouse gases produced on Earth, more than all the greenhouse gas emissions from all the different forms of transport on Earth.

Part of this ancient rainforest has been cut down so that a cattle ranch can be built.

This poster by the Vegetarian Society is encouraging people to stop eating meat because of its effect on the environment.

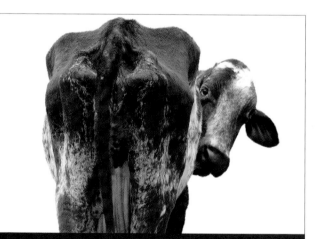

SILENT BUT DEADLY

Did you know that farmed animals produce more greenhouse gas emissions (18%) than the world's entire transport system (13.5%)? Or that nitrous oxide from animal manure is around 300 times as damaging to the climate as carbon dioxide? Or that methane (cow and sheep farts/burps to you and me) has 23 times the global warming impact of carbon dioxide?

Makes you think doesn't it?

The only genuine way to cut down on these harmful emissions is to stop eating meat.

Find out the facts about 'Why it's green to go vegetarian' at www.vegsoc.org/environment, or order your free booklet on 0161 925 2000, green@vegsoc.org

It's not just a lot of hot air.

Reference: Food and Agriculture Organisation of the United Nations, 2006. Livestock's Long Shadow – Environmental Issues and Options

Vegetarian SOCIETY

Green farming

Some people argue that it is possible to farm animals and look after the environment at the same time. Organic farmers try to use traditional farming methods that do not damage animal habitats or local wildlife. They don't use artificial chemicals.

Overfishing

Many of the world's oceans have been overfished. Stocks of some species of fish are now so low that they may die out. Some countries have set a limit on how many fish can be caught in their waters. Some vegetarians think we need to stop eating so many fish.

RESEARCH IT YOURSELF

Find out about: the work of the Marine Stewardship Council. Use their website to find out which fish are not endangered.

Some species of fish, for example North Sea cod, are in danger because too many have been fished, too quickly.

ROLE PLAY: SO WHAT IF A FISH IS HUNTED TO EXTINCTION?

Here are two different people's opinions on conservation. Can you take one of their arguments and follow it through?

1

"Extinctions have happened throughout history; think about the dinosaurs. So what if a species is hunted to extinction? Another one will take its place."

Grandparent, Dennis Frampton

2

"We should respect animals and their habitats. We have no right to destroy any living species. Nothing exactly like it will exist again."

Conservationist, Magda Podowski

Feeding the world

Some people become vegetarian because they believe that the world is facing a food crisis. The population of the world is rising but there is a limited amount of land for farming. Farming animals is a much less efficient use of that land than growing crops. Crops do not use up as much of the world's valuable water and energy supplies.

Many crops are grown to feed animals, not humans. Precious land and water are used to produce these crops.

People in poorer countries often have no choice about being vegetarian. Meat is too expensive, so they live on cheaper foods, such as rice.

Too land hungry?

Almost three-quarters of all farmland is used to raise animals — that's a third of the land surface of the world. Over a third of all cereal crops go to feed those animals. Some vegetarians ask whether it is right to use so much land for this purpose. Meat-eaters may reply that as long as people want to eat meat, land should be used in this way.

Rising demand

As some countries develop and become wealthier, for example India and China, more and more people are choosing to eat meat. The rise in demand for meat is a problem building up for the future. Some vegetarians believe the answer is for everyone to stop eating meat. But others say people have the right to eat what they like.

Farming animals uses up natural resources, such as water.

Do you agree with either of these people or do you have a different view?

1

"Rich countries shouldn't tell poorer ones not to eat meat, unless they are prepared to stop eating it themselves. People should be left to make their own decisions."

Journalist, Ruma Kazi

2

"The world doesn't have the resources to allow everyone to eat meat, whether they want to or not. Everyone, everywhere should become vegetarian to solve the world food crisis."

Teacher, Liam Connor

IN FOCUS

Water shortages

Farming animals uses more water than farming crops — animals drink water, and farmers need to water crops grown to feed their animals. A kilogram of wheat can be grown using much less water than it takes to produce a kilogram of meat. In some countries water is very scarce, so farm animals may even compete with humans for water.

YOUR CALL You know that eating meat uses up much more of the Earth's resources then being vegetarian. Does this make you want to eat less meat, or become a vegetarian?

The healthy choice?

Some people choose to be vegetarian because they believe it is healthier. A vegetarian diet of fresh fruit, vegetables, pulses and cereals, without too much cheese and milk, can be very good for you. However, it is harder for vegetarians to plan a diet that includes all the nutrients they need.

The right balance?

Most vegetarian foods, for example fruits, nuts, pulses and vegetables, provide fibre, protein, vitamins and minerals. They are also low in fat. However, vegetarians must eat the right amounts of each type of food.

They may need a doctor's advice, to help them plan their diet. For example, when girls start their periods, they need almost twice as much iron as boys of the same age, or they may become anaemic. See page 6 for good sources of iron.

ARGUMENTS FOR AND AGAINST VEGETARIAN DIETS

FOR!

AGAINST!

- Doctors recommend diets that are low in fat and high in fibre. The vegetarian diet ticks both of these boxes.
- Vegetarians are less likely to suffer from heart disease, obesity, diabetes and some forms of cancer.
- Fruit and vegetables contain chemicals called antioxidants, which help to stop damage to cells in the body. This may prevent some diseases, such as cancer.

- You need to eat enough of the right kinds of food to stay healthy. This can be more difficult for vegetarians than meat-eaters.
- Meat is a good source of iron. If people do not have enough iron in their diet, they may develop anaemia.
- Nut allergies are increasingly common. A vegetarian with a nut allergy may not have enough protein in their diet.

A diet that is properly balanced will keep you fit and healthy, whether it is vegetarian or not.

? Dilemma:

Anna is a vegetarian, and she is worried about her parents. Heart disease runs in the family, and she thinks her parents would live longer if they became vegetarians. But Anna's parents have never liked her being a vegetarian. What should Anna do?

IN FOCUS

Athletic ability

Vegetarians have low levels of iron and a compound called carnosine, which is found in meat. This may affect how well they do at athletics. However, Edwin Moses is a life-long vegetarian and a world famous athlete. He won two Olympic gold medals for the hurdles.

Edwin Moses was a successful American athlete who is a life-long vegetarian.

A balanced diet

It is not enough for vegetarians to 'leave meat off the plate'. They need to change the way they eat, to make sure they have enough protein, vitamins and minerals, carbohydrate, fibre and fat in their diet. Some people don't want to become vegetarian because they think that planning a balanced vegetarian diet will take too much time and effort.

A healthy vegetarian meal is very tasty, but preparing some vegetarian food takes a long time.

Vegetarian ingredients

Vegetarian food should use ingredients from the following groups: cereals and grains; pulses, nuts and seeds; fruit and vegetables; soya or dairy products. Preparing some vegetarian dishes can be time-consuming as beans, for example, may need to be soaked before they are cooked. However, vegetarians say the end result is well worth it! Cookbooks offer many ideas for recipes.

IN FOCUS

Taking supplements

Supplements should only be taken if a particular nutrient is missing from your diet. They are not needed if you have a balanced diet. Vegans, however, should make sure they get enough vitamin B12, vitamin D and calcium. They may need to take supplements of these nutrients.

YOUR CALL You want to become a vegetarian but don't like vegetables. What should you do?

ROLE PLAY: WHICH DIET IS BETTER?

These two people have strong views about vegetarian food. Who is right?

1

"Meat-eaters can eat vegetarian food, but it doesn't work the other way round. This means meat-eaters have more choice than vegetarians, so it is better not to have a vegetarian diet."

Chef, Leroy Jackson

2

"Vegetarian food can be delicious. There are many different types of tasty beans, seeds, lentils and nuts. Vegetarians bother to experiment with these foods, but meat-eaters usually don't."

Health shop owner, Jasmin Patel

RESEARCH IT YOURSELF

Find out about these special vegetarian food products: soya, tofu, Quorn and TVP (textured vegetable protein).

Protein

Meat, fish, eggs and dairy products are good sources of protein, but none of these are eaten by vegans. This means that vegans must get their protein from pulses (such as lentils, chickpeas and beans) and vegetarian products in shops, including tofu and Quorn. If vegans don't eat enough protein, they may become ill. Some people decide not to become vegan for this reason.

We should eat at least five portions of fruit and vegetables a day as part of a balanced diet. This should be easy for vegetarians.

Vegetarian children

Children must get enough essential nutrients from the food they eat, to help them grow. Some doctors say that a vegetarian diet is good for children, but others disagree, saying it is very hard to get the balance of nutrients just right. A healthy diet is vital for babies and children. It protects them against illness, and helps them grow strong bones and teeth, firm muscles and healthy tissues.

The best start?

Some people argue that children in developed countries eat far too much fat and sugar, and not enough fibre, iron and calcium. They say that vegetarian children start with an advantage, as their diet is usually lower in fat and higher in fibre. A vegetarian diet can provide all the nutrients a child needs. However, this diet must be carefully planned by an adult.

Special supplements

If parents want to bring up children as vegetarians, they must be aware of the nutrients that they may lack and provide proper supplements if necessary. Children need lots of protein in their diet, so that their bones, muscles and vital organs can grow properly. Meat is a very good source of protein, so if it is cut out of a child's diet, it is important to find a suitable substitute.

Nut allergies

Nuts are packed with protein and essential nutrients, but if there is a family history of nut-allergy, it is best to avoid all nuts until the child is over three years old. Whole nuts should not be given to babies and young children, as they may make them choke.

If a growing child has a poor diet, such as a high fat diet, the effects can last long into their adult life and be hard to put right.

IN FOCUS

Life vegetarians

Some people were born into vegetarian families and have been brought up on a vegetarian diet and never eaten meat. They are called 'life vegetarians'. This is becoming more common, as more vegetarians are growing up and having families of their own.

ROLE PLAY: SHOULD CHILDREN HAVE A CHOICE?

These people don't agree about whether children should be brought up as vegetarians. Can you take one of their arguments and follow it through?

1

"Parents should let their children make their own decisions. Being a vegetarian is all about choice. If a child has never eaten meat, they have not actually chosen to be vegetarian."

Youth worker, Jordan Green

2

"Vegetarians believe that eating meat is wrong, so they don't want their children to eat it either. If they bring their children up as vegetarians, they are giving them the best start."

Parent, Fiona Hardcastle

Read the label

Some ingredients that are 'hidden' in foods are not suitable for vegetarians. For example, animal fats are found in many biscuits, cakes, bread and desserts. Vegetarians try not to eat foods that were made using animal products. This is not easy to do, because it is not always obvious.

Unsuitable foods

Many 'innocent' looking foods are a problem for vegetarians. Biscuits, chips and ice cream may contain animal fats, and crisps and chocolate often contain whey (see below). Vegetarians should read the label on food packaging to check the ingredients before they eat the food. This may be difficult to do, especially if you are out at a party.

Curds and whey

In cheese-making, an animal product called rennet is used to create curds and whey. The curds become the cheese and the whey is used in cakes, biscuits and some margarines. Vegetarian cheese is made using a different process. Vegetarians should avoid foods made with whey unless it states that it is suitable for vegetarians.

IN FOCUS

Sweets and jellies

If you want to be vegetarian, you may have to give up some types of sweet. Gelatine, which is used to make many sweets and jellies, is made from boiled down animal skin and bones. Other ingredients used in sweets include some E numbers, such as E120 (a red food colouring), which is made from crushed insects.

Vegetarians should check that the cheese label says 'Suitable for vegetarians'.

Many sweets contain gelatine, which is an animal product.

RESEARCH IT YOURSELF

Find out about products that are not suitable for vegetarians:

animal rennet, glycerine, gelatine, whey.

YOUR CALL Your vegetarian friend is eating sweets that you know contain gelatine. Should you tell her and embarrass her in front of the group you are with?

ROLE PLAY: WHAT IS A 'TRUE' VEGETARIAN?

These two people disagree about how far they should go to be vegetarians. Can you take one of their arguments and follow it through?

1 "Vegetarians who don't bother to read labels on food are not true vegetarians. Many foods and snacks contain ingredients made from animal products. Eating them is just as bad as eating meat."

Student, Maya Swinton

2 "It's too much fuss to check every label before you eat something, and it's not possible anyway. Vegetarians shouldn't have to feel guilty about everything they eat. They don't eat meat, which is the main thing."

Parent, Ben Jones

Going vegetarian

It is easier to become a vegetarian now than it was in the past. There is more vegetarian food in the shops, many restaurants have vegetarian dishes, and most school canteens have a vegetarian option. However, as a growing child, you do need to make sure that you eat a healthy, balanced diet, vegetarian or not.

It is becoming much easier to find vegetarian food, even when you are out for the day.

Do your homework

If you want to become a vegetarian, talk to vegetarians you know, and borrow books from the library to find out about vegetarianism. You could also look up The Vegetarian Society on the Internet. Try to explain to friends and family about your decision, without getting cross.

Get advice

Some people think children shouldn't be vegetarians, because they are still growing. If you want to be a vegetarian, find out what you need to eat to have a balanced diet. You could ask your doctor for some advice.

YOUR CALL You have decided to become a vegetarian but your parents want you to carry on eating meat. Should you give up and do as they say, try to convince them to change their diet or learn to cook vegetarian dishes yourself?

Chloe's mum disagrees with Chloe's decision to become a vegetarian. Can you take one of their arguments and follow it through?

1

"I don't want to cook special meals for Chloe. She should eat the same food as the rest of the family. She's only ten years old; she can eat what she likes when she's old enough to cook for herself."

Parent, Sonia Bentley

2

"It's my body, and it's my choice what I eat. I've thought carefully about it, and I don't want to eat meat anymore."

Chloe Bentley

RESEARCH IT YOURSELF

Find out about the five food groups: protein, vitamins and minerals, fibre, carbohydrate and fat. Also find out what types of vegetarian foods fall into each group. Make sure you eat some from each group every week.

If you want to become a vegetarian, offer to help with any extra shopping and cooking.

Clothes and make-up

Vegetarians often have strong views on materials made with animal products. They may refuse to wear leather clothes or shoes, and won't wear anything made from animal fur. Fortunately, there are man-made alternatives to both leather and fur. Make-up and skin products can also be a problem for vegetarians. They may not be happy to use products that have been tested on animals.

Many things we buy and use are made from leather.

ROLE PLAY: SHOULD VEGETARIANS WEAR LEATHER?

Some people disagree about how far vegetarians should go to make their point. What do you think?

1

"If vegetarians care about animals, they shouldn't wear or use leather. Animals are killed to make leather."

Veterinary nurse, Sabine Dupont

2

"Vegetarians shouldn't feel guilty about wearing leather. The fact they don't eat meat shows they care about what happens to animals."

Fashion designer, Max Tallis

Leather goods

Leather is made from the skin of animals, mostly cows. Soft leather comes from calves and the softest leather of all is made from the skins of unborn calves. Other animals that are used for leather include deer, alligators, crocodiles, toads, kangaroos, lizards, snakes and seals. Some of these are endangered species. Many vegetarians believe that it is wrong to wear leather, as this supports the meat industry which is paid for the skins. Others feel differently as the animal skins would otherwise go to waste.

Forget fur

Vegetarians are sometimes involved in protests against the fur trade. Animals are either hunted or farmed for their fur, and both methods involve cruelty. Thanks to an anti-fur campaign in the 1980s, many people stopped wearing real fur. Hunting endangered animals for their fur, such as big cats, has been banned.

Tested on animals

Many vegetarians will not buy cosmetic products, for example shampoos, make-up and skin creams, that were tested on animals. It is possible to buy cosmetics that were made without animal testing. The packaging will usually say if this is the case.

Many people, not just vegetarians, think it is wrong to make clothes and fashion accessories with animal fur.

Make-up is often tested on animals before it reaches the shops, to check it is safe for people to use.

RESEARCH IT YOURSELF

Find out about some endangered species that are used to make leather goods and the efforts that are being made to protect them:
alligators, crocodiles, snakes, toads.

YOUR CALL You are given a soft leather bag as a present. You don't agree with how leather is made, so should you give the present back and explain why, or give it away?

Extreme vegetarians

Some people take the vegetarian diet to extremes, cutting many different types of food out of their daily meals. For example, fruitarians mainly eat fruit, and people who follow macrobiotic diets gradually cut out most types of food from their diet. Extreme vegetarians like this must take vitamin and mineral supplements to stay healthy.

Fruitarians

Fruitarians follow a vegan diet, but also avoid processed and cooked food. They leave pulses and cereals out of their diet. A fruitarian diet is mainly made up of raw and dried fruits, nuts, honey and olive oil. A fruitarian diet contains lots of sugar, which can be bad for people's teeth.

Do fruitarians eat vegetables?

As well as all the usual kinds of fruit, fruitarians think of avocados, cucumbers, tomatoes, paprika, olives, squash and all kinds of berries as 'fruits'. They don't cook their food, to keep all the vitamins, minerals and enzymes well preserved in the fruit.

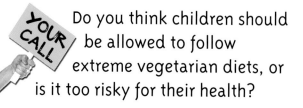

Do you think children should be allowed to follow extreme vegetarian diets, or is it too risky for their health?

Fruitarians eat organic fruits when they are in season. This means they may eat lots of one kind of fruit at a time.

Raw vegan diets are made up of three food groups: sweet fruit, high-fat plants and green leafy vegetables.

Raw food diet

Vegans who follow a raw food diet cut out all cooked, processed and refined foods from their diet. They believe that cooking food destroys enzymes, vitamins and minerals. People on a raw vegan diet often lose weight, due to the lack of calories in the food they eat. It is very hard to include all the nutrients the body needs in a raw vegan diet.

RESEARCH IT YOURSELF

Find out more about the following: vitamins, minerals, calories, enzymes.

Steve Jobs helped set up Apple, the international computer company, about 30 years ago. He was a fruitarian at the time.

IN FOCUS

Macrobiotic diets

There are ten 'levels' in a macrobiotic diet, and at each level, different food types are cut out. Animal products are gradually removed, until the diet is vegetarian. But then, fruit and vegetables are also removed, until at the highest level, the diet consists only of brown rice. Fluids may also be restricted. High level macrobiotic diets can be bad for your health. People who follow these diets often do so for religious or philosophical reasons.

Vegetarianism around the world

Vegetarianism has been practised for centuries around the world, for religious and cultural reasons. Some people are vegetarian because their religion forbids them to eat meat. Others may be vegetarian because meat is too expensive, or is simply not available where they live.

The Hindu religion encourages people to respect animals, and not to eat meat. Cows are sacred.

Vegetarian religions

People may be vegetarian because of their religious beliefs, for example if they are Buddhist or Hindu. Seventh-Day Adventists and some Rastafarians are also vegetarian. Certain religions ask people not to eat some types of meat — Jews and Muslims, for example, do not eat pork. Some people believe it is wrong for religions to tell us what we should or shouldn't eat.

Vegetarianism in the West

In Western countries, vegetarianism became popular in the second half of the 20th century. It was linked with 'alternative' lifestyles, for example the way of life of hippies. However, vegetarianism has slowly become a much more acceptable choice and a much easier diet to follow. People who want to be vegetarians are not seen as strange or unusual in any way.

A vegetarian thali – a south Indian meal consisting of several small dishes, rice and bread.

Free choice

There are many arguments in favour of vegetarianism, but not everyone is convinced. People who like eating meat may not be prepared to change their diet, or they may think it is good to farm animals. Everyone has the right to their own point of view. No one should be forced to become a vegetarian, just as no vegetarian should be forced to eat meat.

Your best friend has become a vegetarian, and is trying to persuade you to become one too. But you are happy eating meat. You understand your friend's arguments, but don't want to change your diet. What should you say to your friend?

IN FOCUS Vegetarian organisations

There are organisations that help people who have chosen to become vegetarians. The Vegetarian Society and The Vegan Society are good sources of information. They have useful websites to answer questions and give helpful advice (see page 31).

RESEARCH IT YOURSELF

Find out about vegetarianism in the following religions:
Hinduism, Buddhism, Rastafarianism, Jainism.

Glossary

Antioxidant	A chemical that helps protect the cells in your body.
Calcium	A kind of mineral you need to have strong bones and teeth.
Calories	Units of energy found in food.
Carbohydrate	A source of energy in a diet, found in sugary and starchy foods.
Cosmetic	A product that people use on their skin or hair to either clean themselves or make themselves more attractive.
Enzyme	A chemical which helps you digest food more easily.
Fibre	A substance, found in cereals, fruits and vegetables, which helps you to digest food.
Free-range	Farmed outside, in natural conditions.
Fruitarian	A person who only eats fruit.
Gelatine	An animal product used to make sweets, jellies and some other foods.
Greenhouse gas	A kind of gas that helps to cause global warming, or climate change.
Intensive farming	A method of farming that produces the most food, in the fastest time, from the smallest amount of land.
Iron	A nutrient you need to have healthy blood.
Macrobiotic diet	A kind of diet that cuts out most foods, except whole grains and beans.
Mineral	A nutrient you need in your diet to stay healthy and strong.
Nutrients	Substances in food that you need to grow properly and stay healthy.
Omnivore	A person or animal with a diet of meat and vegetables.
Organic farming	A farming method that uses natural fertilisers and avoids chemicals.
Poultry	Birds that are kept for their eggs and meat.
Processed food	Food that is treated in factories, often to keep it fresh.
Protein	An essential nutrient that keeps you healthy and helps you grow.
Pulses	Plants that produce seeds in pods, for example peas and beans.
Raw food	Food that has not been processed or cooked.
Refined food	Food that has been treated to remove unwanted parts, including some healthy nutrients.
Rennet	An animal product that is used to make cheese.
Soya	A kind of bean that is used to make some vegetarian food.
Supplements	Nutrients that are added to a diet to make up for a gap, or deficiency.
Vegan	A strict vegetarian who cuts all dairy foods out of their diet.
Vegetarian	Someone who does not eat meat, poultry, fish or any animal product.
Vitamin	A substance in food you need to keep healthy.

Further information

Websites

Note to parents and teachers: Every effort has been made by the Publishers to ensure that these websites are suitable for children, that they are of the highest educational value, and that they contain no inappropriate or offensive material. However, because of the nature of the Internet, it is impossible to guarantee that the contents of these sites will not be altered. We strongly advise that Internet access is supervised by a responsible adult.

Index